Mediterranean cooking

CARLA CAPALBO

SIMON & SCHUSTER
A VIACOM COMPANY

First published in Great Britain by Martin Books, 1997
a division of Simon & Schuster
A Viacom Company

Martin Books, Grafton House, 64 Maids Causeway
Cambridge CB5 8DD

First published 1997
ISBN 0 85941 948 7

Design and typesetting: Jane Humphrey
Photography: Steve Baxter
Food stylist: Jane Stevenson
Styling: Roisin Nield

Printed and bound in Italy

Picture Credits: page 8 Image Bank; pages 16-17 Robert Harding Picture Library;
pages 30-1 and 58 S.O.A; pages 44-5 Photonica

Le Creuset UK Ltd
4 Stephenson Close
East Portway
Andover
Hants SP10 3RU

A Division of The Le Creuset Group

On the front cover; *Pan-fried Prawns with Garlic, Herbs & Basil Mayonnaise,
page 18*

CONTENTS

FOREWORD

The Romans referred to the Mediterranean sea as the 'mare nostrum' – our sea, and since those early times its importance politically and as a hub of maritime trade has changed little. Today, as then, the sea is at the heart of the region we know as 'the Mediterranean'.

This sea is only open at its western end and is linked to the Atlantic ocean by the Strait of Gibraltar. The countries along its vast coastline have, for centuries, relied on its bounty, whether it be the harvest from the sea itself, the ingredients and spices transported across its waters, or the lush fruits and vegetables which flourish in its gentle climate; these foods have formed the basis of traditional Mediterranean cooking.

Like Mediterranean cooking, Le Creuset has its own traditions which date back to the mid 1500s. Evolving over the years, Le Creuset cast-iron cookware has become known as the cookware for real cooks, offering them unsurpassed flexibility of use, whether for quick searing of meats on a grill, simmering sauces slowly and gently over many hours to achieve the ultimate flavour, or for baking the lightest of cakes and pastries. There is a Le Creuset dish for almost any recipe you could wish to cook.

Cast iron is an ideal material for cookware. It heats slowly and evenly and once hot requires a minimum of heat to maintain cooking temperatures. Once the food is cooked Le Creuset's heat-retaining qualities allow for a relaxed style of eating because second servings are kept hot without spoiling.

Centuries ago cast-iron cooking pots were used over charcoal fires. Today's heat sources are much more diverse, but Le Creuset can be used with ease on them all; and on an improvised beach fire, or on the barbecue at home, your cast-iron pot will still cook as reliably as its forerunners did in earlier days. Most pieces work equally well on the hob, under the grill, or in the oven, and their elegant styling makes them perfect for table serving too. Their vibrant colours of volcanic orange, cerise red, green, and hues of yellow and blue make them ideal partners to any kitchen or dining colour scheme.

The traditions of Mediterranean cookery are legendary but simple. The recipes in this book illustrate the diversity of ingredients used throughout the region, while cooking in cast iron helps you bring out the true flavours of the Mediterranean.

Bon Appetit!
Le Creuset

INTRODUCTION

If I close my eyes and think of the Mediterranean, I think of light and warmth, colour and scents, aromas and flavours. I think of the view from Matisse's windows in Nice: palm trees and azure sky, or the multi-coloured mosaics of Gaudi's spires in Barcelona.

The Mediterranean is a sum of impressions, of sensations, of tastes. It is the memory of sweet figs plucked from the tree, still warm from the sun, of spiky sea urchins cracked against the rocks and eaten raw, of old men dressed in black, sitting in chairs around a piazza. It is olive groves and vineyards, lemon trees and orange blossom, jasmine and bougainvillea. It is the sight, in spring, of old women armed with bags scouring the roadsides for wild greens, bitter and astringent, and again in autumn, combing the woods for mushrooms: *porcino, cèpe, siureny*. The names may change with each country but the rituals remain the same.

The Mediterranean is a sum of cultures. The great blue sea was crossed and crossed again by conquerors and colonisers: the Greeks to Sicily, the Spanish to Genoa, the Romans to Spain, the Moors to Spain, to Sicily and back. Cultures were imposed, implanted, interchanged. So were foods. The Sicilians still eat *cùscusu*, a close cousin to its North African namesake, *couscous*; the Moorish legacy included a passion for sweets, which both the Sicilians and the Spanish now share. The cuisine of Nice was heavily influenced by its Sardinian invaders – many of its dishes are distinctly Italian. Venice was rich with oriental spices.

The countries surrounding the sea share a landscape whose features have determined their inhabitants' way of life – and their way of eating. Arid but rarely barren, the rocky lands of intensely hot, long summers (and often not such gentle winters) favour olives and eucalyptus, palms and grape vines, wild herbs and their foragers: goats and sheep. Much of the southern Mediterranean is covered with dense *macchia mediterranea,* the bushy scrub that flowers so magically in spring and lends the summer its aromatic air. Fennel and rosemary, juniper and thyme, prickly pear and fig grow wild.

In the fields, sun-lovers thrive: aubergine and tomatoes, peppers and courgettes, garlic and basil. These are the stars of a healthy cuisine of decisive flavours, simply cooked. For the true Mediterranean food has humble origins. Before the days of refrigerated transport or imported fertilisers, local people relied on the few vegetables and fruits that could be grown with little water, and on whatever could be fished from the sea or kept on the land. Accents were provided by salt-dried capers, anchovies and olives, by chilli, rosemary and sage. Pure golden olive oil was as elemental as water or wine.

A trip to the local market in France or Spain, Italy or Morocco reveals that things have changed, yet stayed the same. Undoubtedly, the range of produce is wider now: the winter Riviera is served by southern Spain and Italy; hot-houses exist everywhere. What has thankfully remained unchanged is each country's (or province's) local specialities, the 'spontaneous' (as the

Italians like to call them) ingredients that determine a region's cuisine: a cluster of four lemons, waiting to be tipped into your bag; bunches of hand-gathered herbs or wild salads, like the fiery rocket that is ten times more piquant than its cultivated counterpart; vats of olives of all colours and sizes. Thankfully, too, many of these foods appear only once a year – when they are naturally in season. Autumn brings grapes, and then chestnuts and mushrooms, pumpkins, game and truffles; spring is the time for tender artichokes and peas, medlars, dandelion and nettles. Nature's rhythms are respected in seasonal dishes that are looked forward to, prepared and then put away until the next year.

A word about extra virgin olive oil

When buying extra virgin olive oil, try to get estate-bottled oil. It may cost a bit more than industrially produced oil but it will more then repay its cost in quality. An aromatic, fruity oil can turn a good meal into a great one. Fine small producers hand-pick and press olives that they have grown themselves, which usually means they have been attentive to each stage of the (necessarily costly) process. Industrial oil is bought in as 'crude extra virgin' from many countries around the Mediterranean, regardless of where the bottler is located. It is always a blend, often including high percentages of seed oils – a fact that the companies are not obliged to declare on the label.

A (personal) word about Le Creuset's pans

My mother bought me my first Le Creuset casserole in the seventies, when I left home to go to university. For me, it was an important symbol of my new autonomy, a keystone in a young woman's beginning to build a home, and a life, for herself. I learned to cook using that pan: from making the simplest spaghetti sauces to mastering the most complex recipes Julia Child could write, it did its job, cheery and orange and indestructible. I still have it. Over the years I have added to it – a gratin dish, a frying-pan, the giant casserole for my first big dinner party – but I must admit I hold a particular affection for that first, small casserole. After all these years, it looks as good as new. We wrote this book together. What more could you ask from a pot?
Carla Capalbo, 1997

This book is dedicated to Gary Copeland and Gary Nikolis.
Many thanks to Janet Copleston, Linda Lumley and Susanna Clarke at Martin Books, and to Sue Cutts at Le Creuset for making it such a pleasure to work on this book, and to my mother, Patricia Lousada, for her help and inspiration with the recipes.

RECIPE NOTES: All teaspoon and tablespoon measurements are level. All eggs are medium unless otherwise stated. Measurements are given in both metric and imperial units. Use either set of quantities, but not a mixture of both, in any one recipe.

AMERICAN AND AUSTRALIAN CONVERSION CHART

	BRITISH	AMERICAN	AUSTRALIAN
teaspoons and tablespoons	1 teaspoon	1 teaspoon	1 teaspoon
	1 tablespoon	1 rounded tablespoon	1 scant tablespoon
	2 tablespoons	2 tablespoons	1½ tablespoons
	3 tablespoons	3 tablespoons	2½ tablespoons
	4 tablespoons	4 tablespoons	3½ tablespoons
	5 tablespoons	5 tablespoons	4½ tablespoons
cup measures for liquids	4 tablespoons	¼ cup	¼ cup
	125 ml	½ cup	½ cup
	250 ml	1 cup	1 cup
	450 ml	2 cups	2 cups
	600 ml	2½ cups	2½ cups
cup measures for solids	225 g butter	1 cup	1 cup
	225 g caster sugar	1 cup	1 cup
	125 g icing sugar	1 cup	1 cup
	225 g flour	2 cups	2 cups
	175 g dried fruit	1 cup	1 cup
	225 g grated hard cheese,		
	such as Parmesan	2 cups	2 cups
	60 g breadcrumbs	½ cup	½ cup
	200 g long-grain rice	1 cup	1 cup
	2 medium onions, chopped	1 cup	1 cup

TO BEGIN

Traditional meals in France, Italy and Spain always offer a well-defined progression of courses. *Antipasti* and *hors d'oeuvres* are taste-whetters, an expected way to begin a full, lengthy dinner. To many Italians, pasta would be unthinkable as a main course. It could only be a *primo*, a first course to precede the meat or fish.

Times have changed, however, and modern meals have become as flexible as our lifestyles: we don't always want, or need, or have time, to prepare three or more courses. What works now are quick, tasty starters that set the mood and are easy to make, like tapas, or an unusual salad, some roast vegetables, an interesting bruschetta. Here is a collection of ideas to get you going, plus some fail-safe recipes – a flavourful gazpacho, a pretty vegetable terrine and a white bean dip with sun-dried tomatoes – in case you are planning that nice long dinner party.

GAZPACHO

Serves 6 Freezing recommended for broth only
Preparation time, broth: 15 minutes + 50 minutes cooking + chilling; garnish: 15 minutes

This is Spain's classic iced summer soup, one of the most refreshing, colourful foods ever invented for a really hot summer's day. It exists in many versions, from the humble to the grand. I like this combination of a chilled winter vegetable broth with its garnish of crisp summer vegetables.

FOR THE BROTH:

1 large onion, chopped
1 garlic clove
3 carrots, diced
2 potatoes, diced
1 or 2 outer leaves from a fennel bulb, diced
2 celery sticks, sliced thinly
3 ripe tomatoes, chopped, plus their stalks
    if they have them
bouquet garni
1 teaspoon salt
2 litres (3½ pints) water

FOR THE GARNISH:

½ cucumber, peeled and diced
3 ripe tomatoes, de-seeded and diced, or a handful of
    cherry tomatoes, diced
1 red or yellow pepper, diced
1 green pepper, diced
3 hard-boiled eggs, chopped (optional)
4 spring onions, chopped finely
1 tablespoon white wine vinegar
6 rounds of French bread, toasted
1 or 2 garlic cloves, halved

extra virgin olive oil (the best you have)
8–10 fresh basil leaves, chopped
salt and freshly ground black pepper

1 Place all the broth ingredients, including the tomato stalks (they have good flavour), in a large, heavy saucepan or casserole. Bring to the boil. Reduce the heat slightly and cook, partially covered, for about 50 minutes, or until the carrots are tender.

2 Strain the broth through a nylon or stainless steel strainer, pressing the vegetables against the strainer to extract as much liquid as possible. Taste for seasoning. Cover and chill for several hours or overnight.

3 Shortly before serving, prepare the cucumber, tomatoes, peppers and eggs, if using, for the garnish, making separate piles of each on a large plate or in separate small bowls. Place the chopped spring onion in a small bowl and moisten with the vinegar. Rub the toasts with the cut garlic cloves before cutting them into small squares. Drizzle with extra virgin olive oil.

4 To serve, give each diner a bowl of the chilled, coral-coloured broth with a little basil sprinkled in the centre. Pass the garnishes and garlic croûtons, letting each person serve themselves.

NOTE: The broth vegetables will make a fine purée for another meal. Just remove the bouquet garni and tomato stalks before passing the vegetables through the medium setting of a food mill or processing gently. Heat well, stir in some butter or olive oil, adjust the seasoning and serve.

HERB-SCENTED VEGETABLE TERRINE

Serves 6–8 Freezing not recommended

Preparation time: 1¼ hours + 45 minutes baking + cooling

This delicately flavoured, pretty green and pink terrine is designed to fit Le Creuset's 1.1-litre (2-pint) terrine exactly. If you are using the larger size, increase the quantities by a quarter. Make the terrine several hours or a day before you wish to serve it, to allow it time to cool. Serve on its own or surrounded by a salad of quartered cherry tomatoes, dressed with a little olive oil and balsamic vinegar.

40 g (1½ oz) dried white breadcrumbs
125 g (4½ oz) fresh spinach, thick stalks removed
100 g (3½ oz) tender green beans, tops and tails removed
275 g (9½ oz) courgettes, trimmed
5 eggs
1½ teaspoons salt
½ teaspoon freshly ground black pepper
a pinch of ground mace or nutmeg
1 tablespoon finely chopped fresh mint
2 tablespoons finely chopped fresh parsley
2 tablespoons finely chopped fresh dill
100 g (3½ oz) Parmesan and/or gruyère cheese, grated
100 g (3½ oz) ham, diced
100 g (3½oz) mozzarella cheese, diced

1 Put a saucepan of water on to boil for blanching the beans and courgettes. Preheat the oven to Gas Mark 4/180°C/350°F. Butter the terrine well and line the bottom with greaseproof paper. As the terrine will be baked in a bain-marie, prepare a pan large and deep enough for it to stand in, with water about halfway up its sides. Fill the bain-marie with the correct amount of water and place in the oven. Spread the breadcrumbs on a baking tray and toast them in the oven as it warms. Remove them when they are golden.

2 Wash the spinach carefully in several changes of water until no grit is left in the basin after the spinach has been lifted out. Spin it dry and chop it finely. Drop the beans and courgettes into the boiling water and blanch for 4 minutes. Drain. Dice. Combine with the chopped spinach.

3 In a large bowl, beat the eggs well. Beat in the seasonings and herbs. Add the toasted breadcrumbs and grated Parmesan and/or gruyère cheeses. Stir in the vegetables. The mixture will be very thick.

4 Spoon about half of the vegetable mixture into the prepared terrine, pushing it down evenly to press out air bubbles. Sprinkle the ham and mozzarella in an even layer on top. Cover with the remaining vegetable mixture. Press it down evenly with the back of a spoon. Put the lid on the terrine, place in the heated bain-marie and bake for 35 minutes. Remove the lid and bake for another 10 minutes.

5 Remove from the oven and allow to cool for 5 minutes. Take a palette knife or other supple knife and run the blade around between the sides of the dish and the vegetable terrine. Allow to cool completely before refrigerating.

6 Unmould the terrine by running a knife around the edges again. Place a platter on top of the terrine and turn them both over. Slice before serving, using a sharp, serrated knife. Serve chilled or at room temperature.

WHITE BEAN AND SUN-DRIED TOMATO DIP

Serves 4–5 Freezing not recommended
Preparation time: 15 minutes soaking + 5 minutes

This dip is great with raw vegetables or on toasted ciabatta bread. It can be made in a flash if you have a can of cannellini beans and a couple of sun-dried tomatoes handy. The result is lighter than hummus, but in the same family. If you can't find plain sun-dried tomatoes, use those preserved in oil, adding enough extra water to reach a smooth consistency.

2 or 3 sun-dried tomatoes
400 g (14 oz) can of cannellini beans, drained and rinsed
2 tablespoons extra virgin olive oil
1 tablespoon fresh lemon juice
1 garlic clove
¼ teaspoon cayenne pepper (optional)
salt and freshly ground black pepper

1 Place the sun-dried tomatoes in a small bowl. Cover with boiling water and leave to soften for about 15 minutes.
2 Put all the other ingredients in the bowl of a food processor. Add the tomatoes and a little of their steeping water. Process to a purée, adding more water as necessary. Season to taste. Refrigerate until needed.

SOME GOOD WAYS TO BEGIN A MEDITERRANEAN MEAL

AFFETTATI are sliced cured meats: salami, prosciutto, bresaola, ham, etc. Serve a mixed platter of your favourites, accompanied by pickled vegetables or vegetables preserved in oil and crusty rolls.

PINZIMONIO is the Italian version of the French crudités: an assortment of raw or blanched vegetables to dip in oil as a start of the meal. They are arranged on a pretty platter around a bowl of fragrant, extra virgin olive oil to which only a bit of salt and pepper has been added. Prepare a selection of fennel, carrot, courgette, olives, peppers, broccoli, celery, cucumber, mushrooms ... and use your best oil!

PARMESAN is delicious sliced into thin flakes and served in a salad. For four people arrange 50 g (1¾ oz) rocket and a few thinly sliced leaves of endive on four pretty plates. Thinly slice an apple and divide that between the four plates. Now take 125 g (4½ oz) large shavings of fresh Parmesan and divide these between the plates (you can easily do this with a potato peeler). Finally drizzle a tablespoon of extra virgin olive oil or a little more over each salad and grind on some pepper.

MOZZARELLA CHEESE from the supermarket lacks lustre. Sprinkle with freshly chopped herbs and fruity olive oil and leave to marinate for 30 minutes before serving. You will really taste the difference.

TORTILLAS or **FRITTATAS** (the Spanish and Italian names respectively) are like slow-cooked, omelettes. For 3–4 people, beat 6 eggs lightly in a bowl. Season with salt and pepper. Stir in 2 sliced onions, softened very slowly in a little olive oil, or 200 g (7 oz) of chopped fresh or frozen spinach or a handful of chopped fresh herbs. Heat 2 tablespoons of extra virgin olive oil in a non-stick skillet. Add the egg mixture and cook over a low heat until the egg starts to puff up and set, about 6 minutes. Do not stir; shake the pan occasionally. Wearing oven gloves, hold a large dish over the pan and invert both of them: the frittata will drop on to the plate. Add a little oil to the pan, if necessary, and slide the frittata back into the pan. Cook on the second side for about 5 minutes more, or until golden underneath. Serve hot or cold, cut in wedges.

BRUSCHETTA is a roasted slice of country-style bread, rubbed with garlic and drizzled with good olive oil. Top it with: chopped ripe tomatoes and basil; a cold seafood salad; some crushed white beans with rosemary-scented oil (below); roasted or grilled vegetables; or olive paste and tuna flakes.

HERB-SCENTED OLIVE OIL is easily made. Gently heat a few tablespoons of extra virgin olive oil in a tiny saucepan. Add a few sprigs of fresh rosemary or sage or some whole garlic cloves. Swirl the oil around for a few minutes so it really picks up the flavour of the herbs.

READY-MADE POLENTA is now readily available. Slice and grill it and serve with olives or vegetable spreads, or any of the bruschetta toppings.

ROASTED VEGETABLES are really easy to make: cut your favourite vegetables into large chunks, toss with olive oil and herbs and roast in a hot oven until golden and tender. Serve hot or cold.

INSTANT COUSCOUS can be used for making cold salads, just like pasta. Cook, toss with a little oil and leave to cool. Mix with chopped tomatoes, cucumber, olives, spring onions and fresh coriander. Dress with a light vinaigrette.

THE SEA

The recipes in this book have been designed to be used in a flexible way. With only a few exceptions they can be made as first or main courses, for lunch or dinner, alone or with others. So I have grouped them as it seemed most natural: fish and shellfish in THE SEA, vegetables, pasta and rice in THE FIELDS, chicken, eggs and meat in THE LAND.

Fish markets in the Mediterranean are always fascinating. Their colourful arrays of delicious and unusual sea creatures often look more exotic than their northern counterparts. You can find everything from the weird to the wonderful, with names that are equally intriguing: *rascasse rouge* (scorpion fish), *hirondelle de mer* (flying fish), *rana pescatrice* (angler-fish), *pez martillo* (hammerhead shark), *gringou* (conger eel). Many species are now available beyond the Mediterranean.

PAN-FRIED PRAWNS WITH GARLIC, HERBS & BASIL MAYONNAISE

Serves 4 Freezing not recommended

Preparation time: 15 minutes + marinating + 10 minutes cooking

A tasty marinade can do wonders for prawns. Serve them hot on toasted rounds of Italian bread as a first course, hot with rice as a main course, or cold with basil mayonnaise.

24 large raw prawns
3 tablespoons fresh lemon juice
5 tablespoons extra virgin olive oil
4 garlic cloves, chopped finely
1 tablespoon chopped fresh dill
1 tablespoon chopped fresh parsley
2 tablespoons chopped fresh basil
coarsely ground black pepper

FOR THE MAYONNAISE:

1 egg yolk
1 teaspoon Dijon-style mustard
1 tablespoon white wine vinegar
250 ml (9 fl oz) olive or vegetable oil
4 tablespoons finely chopped fresh basil
salt and freshly ground black pepper

1 Peel the prawns, if necessary. De-vein them using a small sharp knife: make a shallow incision along the centre of the back to reveal the long black vein. Pull it out and discard it.

2 Make the marinade by combining the lemon juice, 3 tablespoons of the oil, the garlic and herbs in a bowl or enamelled gratin dish. Season with pepper. Add the prawns, stirring to cover them with the marinade. Cover the bowl with cling film and refrigerate for 2 hours or more.

3 To make the mayonnaise, combine the egg yolk, mustard and vinegar in a bowl. Beat vigorously with a small whisk as you add the oil drop by drop at first and then in a slow, steady stream. When all the oil has been added and the mayonnaise is thick and smooth, beat in the basil. Alternatively, make the mayonnaise in a food processor. Briefly process the yolk, mustard, vinegar and seasonings. With the motor running, add the oil in through the funnel in a slow, steady stream, until thick and smooth. Add the basil and process very briefly, to mix. Taste for and adjust the seasoning. Cover and chill until needed.

4 Heat the remaining 2 tablespoons of olive oil in a cast-iron skillet or frying-pan. Spoon in as much of the marinade as you can, and cook over a medium heat for 3–4 minutes or until the garlic begins to soften. Add the prawns and cook for 4–5 minutes, turning them over as they become pink. Remove from the heat and serve hot or turn into a dish and allow to cool.

RED MULLET WITH FENNEL-SEED TOMATO SAUCE

Serves 4 Freezing not recommended
Preparation time: 20 minutes + 20 minutes cooking

This dish is a speciality of Livorno, the Tuscan port; the subtly flavoured mullet are fished in the local Tyrrhenian sea. Red mullet are never very large, so you may want to serve them as a first course; or serve two per person to big eaters.

FOR THE TOMATO SAUCE:

2 tablespoons extra virgin olive oil
1 red onion, about 100 g (3½ oz), chopped finely
3 ripe tomatoes, about 350 g (12 oz), peeled and chopped
½ teaspoon salt

FOR THE FISH:

4 red mullet, about 150 g (5½ oz) each, gutted and scaled
plain flour, seasoned with a little salt
2 tablespoons extra virgin olive oil
1 garlic clove
¼ teaspoon fennel seeds
2 teaspoons very finely chopped fresh parsley

1 Make the tomato sauce. Heat the oil in a medium-sized, heavy-based saucepan. Add the onion and cook over a low heat until it is soft and golden, about 10 minutes. Add the tomatoes and salt and cook for 7–8 minutes more, or until the tomatoes are soft. Purée the sauce in a blender or food processor.

2 Rinse the fish in cool water. Pat dry with paper towels. Roll in the flour, shaking off any excess. Heat the oil with the garlic clove in a non-stick cast-iron frying-pan that is large enough to fit all the fish in one layer. When it is hot, add the fish and cook until golden and soft on one side, 7–8 minutes. Carefully turn the fish over. Cook for 2–3 minutes more before adding the tomato sauce to the pan, spooning it over and between the fish. Sprinkle with the fennel seeds. Shake the pan to distribute the sauce and continue cooking until the sauce is bubbling and the fish is cooked, about 10 minutes more. Sprinkle delicately with parsley and serve, right from the pan.

NOTE: Traditionally pepper is not used in this dish so that the delicate flavour of the fish and the perfume of the fennel seeds are not overpowered.

MIXED FISH SOUP

Serves 6 Freezing not recommended

Preparation time, broth: 15 minutes + 1 hour cooking; soup: 15 minutes + 25 minutes cooking

The Mediterranean's wide assortment of native fish has given rise to an equally wide variety of mixed fish soups, from bouillabaisse to *sopa de mariscos*. Not all of its wonderful sea-creatures are available in Britain but a good, characteristic soup can be made nonetheless.

FOR THE BROTH:

1 onion, chopped

1 carrot, sliced

1 celery stick, sliced

a couple of outer leaves from a fennel bulb, sliced

3 ripe tomatoes, chopped

450 g (1 lb) white fish bones and heads, gills removed

bouquet garni

7 or 8 peppercorns

1.5 litres (2¾ pints) water

FOR THE SOUP:

250 ml (9 fl oz) white wine

450 g (1 lb) mussels, scrubbed, beards removed

4 tablespoons extra virgin olive oil

2 whites of leek, sliced finely

1 carrot, sliced very finely

1 medium celery stick, sliced very finely

2 ripe tomatoes, peeled, de-seeded and chopped finely

2 garlic cloves, chopped finely

1 small, fresh red chilli, chopped finely (optional)

3 tablespoons finely chopped fresh parsley

175 g (6 oz) small cuttlefish or squid, (fresh or frozen), sacs removed, cut into rings

900 g (2 lb) assorted filleted fish, e.g. hake, scorpion

fish (rascasse), monkfish or angler-fish, dogfish, eel, etc. cut into bite-sized pieces

115 g (4 oz) prawns, shelled and de-veined

salt and freshly ground black pepper

rounds of French bread, toasted

1 garlic clove, halved

1 Make the broth by combining all the ingredients for it in a large casserole or saucepan. If you are using unpeeled prawns, peel them and add their shells to the other ingredients. Bring to the boil and cook, partially covered, for about an hour.

2 Strain the broth through a nylon sieve, pressing the vegetables to squeeze out all their flavour. Set the broth aside to cool if not using right away; refrigerate, if necessary. Reheat the broth to simmering when you begin to make the soup.

3 Preheat the oven to Gas Mark 4/180°C/350°F. Place the wine in a medium-sized saucepan with the mussels, discarding any that do not close when sharply tapped. Cover and cook over a high heat until the mussels open, about 5 minutes. Remove from the heat. Lift the mussels out, pouring their liquid back into the pan. Discard any that do not open or are cracked. Strain the liquid through two layers of fine, dampened muslin and reserve. Set the mussels aside.

4 Prepare the toasts by laying out rounds of French bread in one layer on a baking sheet and bake until golden. Before serving, rub each toast with a cut clove of garlic.

5 In the clean large casserole heat the olive oil. Stir in

the leek, carrot and celery. Cook and stir over a low to medium heat until the vegetables soften, about 7–8 minutes. Stir in the tomatoes, garlic, optional chilli and parsley. Cook for 2–3 minutes more. Add the reserved mussel liquid, raise the heat and boil until the liquid reduces slightly. Pour in the broth and bring to the boil.

6 If the squid or cuttle fish you are using are frozen, drop them into the soup. Cook for 2–3 minutes. (If they are fresh, add them later with the prawns, as they will need less cooking time.) Add the fish pieces and cook for 5 minutes. Stir in the prawns and fresh cuttlefish or squid pieces, if using. Cook for 2–3 minutes more. Taste for and adjust the seasoning. Stir in the mussels in their shells and bring the soup back to the boil before serving.

7 Place one or two rounds of toasted French bread in the bottom of each soup bowl. Serve each guest an assortment of fish pieces and a ladleful of broth.

TUNA STEAK IN A CAPER-SAGE CRUST

Serves 2 Freezing not recommended
Preparation time: 10 minutes + 10 minutes cooking

Any of the firm-fleshed fish sold in 'steaks' – swordfish, dogfish, grouper – can be used instead of tuna in this recipe.

4 tablespoons capers, rinsed
6 or 7 fresh sage leaves
6 tablespoons dried white breadcrumbs
1 egg
2 tuna steaks, about 1.5 cm (⅝ inch) thick
25 g (1 oz) butter
2 tablespoons olive oil
salt and freshly ground black pepper
lemon wedges, to serve

1 Finely chop the capers and sage leaves. Combine them with the breadcrumbs on a flat plate. Beat the egg in a shallow bowl. Season with salt and pepper.

2 Dry the fish steaks with paper towels. Dip them first in the egg and then in the flavoured crumbs, patting them with your fingers to make an even coat.

3 Heat the butter and oil in a cast-iron skillet large enough to hold the steaks side by side. When the butter is bubbling, lay the fish in the pan and cook over a medium heat until golden, about 5 minutes. Turn carefully and cook on the other side for about 5 minutes more. Serve immediately with lemon wedges.

BAKED MUSSELS WITH POTATOES AND TOMATOES

Serves 4 as a starter or 2–3 as a main course Freezing not recommended
Preparation time: 45 minutes + 1½ hours baking

This rustic dish is perhaps the most quintessentially Mediterranean in this book. It is a recipe from southern Italy's *cucina povera* ('peasant cooking'), made by the local fishermen's wives out of next to nothing – mussels (gathered freely along the rocky shore) and a few garden vegetables. The result is an irresistibly delicious colourful concoction, flavoured with the area's signature ingredients: garlic, fruity olive oil and herbs.

700 g (1 lb 9 oz) live mussels
400 g (14 oz) potatoes, peeled and sliced very thinly
1 red onion, sliced very thinly
3 tablespoons finely chopped fresh parsley
400 g (14 oz) can of peeled plum tomatoes
3 tablespoons extra virgin olive oil
2–3 garlic cloves, chopped finely
3 tablespoons dried white breadcrumbs
freshly ground black pepper

1 Preheat the oven to Gas Mark 2/150°C/300°F. Lightly rub a heavy oven dish at least 5 cm (2 inches) deep with a little olive oil (Le Creuset's rectangular 30 x 21 cm/12 x 8¼-inch dish is the perfect size).

2 Scrub the mussels well with a small, stiff brush under cold running water. Use a sharp little knife to cut off the 'beards'. Place the mussels in a covered saucepan over a medium heat until they open, about 6–7 minutes. Remove the saucepan from the heat and discard any that have not opened.

3 Cover the bottom of the oven dish with a layer of potato slices, overlapping as little as possible. Use about half of the onion slices to make a layer on top of the potato. Sprinkle with a little parsley and black pepper. Use about half of the tomatoes in the can for this layer: pull the tomatoes out, opening them and letting the juice fall back into the can. Break or chop into pieces and scatter over the onions. Drizzle with 1 tablespoon of the oil.

4 Pull the mussels out of the saucepan one at a time, breaking off the empty half shell and discarding it. (Discard any mussels that have not opened or have badly cracked shells.) Make an even layer of mussels in the half shell (with the mussel facing up) on top of the vegetables in the dish. Use about half of the mussels for this layer. Sprinkle with half of the garlic and a little more parsley. Cover with another layer of potatoes and the remaining onions. Drizzle with 1 tablespoon of oil.

5 Arrange the remaining mussels in a layer. Sprinkle with the remaining garlic. Tilt the saucepan used for opening the mussels and carefully skim off 3–4 tablespoons of the mussels' liquid from the top (the bottom may be gritty), spooning it over the mussels in the dish. Top with a final layer of potatoes, placing a slice over each mussel like a blanket. Scatter with the remaining parsley and tomato pieces, as well as 4 tablespoons of the tomato juice from the can. Sprinkle with black pepper and the breadcrumbs. Drizzle with the remaining oil. Place, uncovered, in the slow oven and bake for 1½ hours, or until the potatoes on top are soft. If the crumbs dry out too much, add a little more oil during baking. Serve hot.

SQUID STUFFED WITH VEGETABLES

Serves 3–4 Freezing not recommended
Preparation time: 1 hour + 20 minutes cooking

Squid or calamari are now readily available in Britain, fresh or frozen. Both work well for this recipe.

200 g (7 oz) small potatoes, peeled
600 g (1 lb 5 oz) squid
65 g (2½ oz) green beans, topped and tailed
60 g (2 oz) peas, fresh or frozen
25 g (1 oz) young spinach leaves, washed and chopped
2 spring onions, chopped
8 black olives, stoned and quartered
1 tablespoon chopped fresh basil
½ teaspoon salt
a small piece of fresh red chilli, chopped finely (optional)
2 tablespoons extra virgin olive oil
2 tablespoons dried white breadcrumbs
FOR THE SAUCE:
2 tablespoons extra virgin olive oil
1 large garlic clove
1 small red onion, chopped very finely
3 tomatoes, peeled, de-seeded and chopped
125 ml (4 fl oz) dry white wine
125 ml (4 fl oz) water
40 g (1½ oz) pine kernels, pounded in a mortar or
   ground lightly in a food processor
salt and freshly ground black pepper

1 Boil the potatoes until just tender. Rinse under cold water. Set one aside and cut the others into 1.5 cm (⅝-inch) cubes.

2 Meanwhile, clean the squid. Cut off the tentacles.

With a small knife, cut through the ring of tentacles and remove the round eye in the centre. Reserve the tentacles. Pull the fins off the lower ends of the sacs and reserve. Pull out and discard everything from inside the sacs, including the long thin transparent quill that resembles plastic. Rinse very well under cold water.

3 Blanch the beans and peas, if fresh, for about 5 minutes. Cool. Chop the beans with the reserved potato. Combine in a bowl, with the peas, spinach, spring onions, olives, basil, salt and chilli, if using. Chop the tentacles and fins of the squid and add them to this stuffing mixture.

4 In a small non-stick frying-pan, heat the oil. Add the stuffing mixture and cook over medium heat for 8–10 minutes. Remove from the heat and stir in the bread-crumbs.

5 Using a tiny spoon, stuff the squid lightly, pushing down the filling to make an even layer. Close the opening, using a cocktail stick. Do not over-stuff the squid since they shrink during cooking.

6 In a buffet casserole or skillet large enough to accommodate all the squid in one layer, make the sauce. Heat the oil with the garlic clove and onion. Sauté gently until the onion is soft and golden. Stir in the tomatoes and cook for 3–4 minutes more. Season. Add the squid to the pan and cook for about 5 minutes on each side. Add the wine, bring to the boil for a minute and then add the water, diced potatoes and pine kernels. Stir gently. Cover the pan and cook for about 15 minutes, turning the squid once or twice. Serve straight from the dish.

THE FIELDS

The hot summer sun breeds strong colours and decisive flavours. The palate of Mediterranean vegetables is deep red, fiery orange, grey-green, violet and black. The intense sweetness of sun-ripened tomatoes is a keystone in the cuisines around the sea; salty olives, aromatic herbs and garlic are their counterpoints. These healthy, appetizing recipes are simple to make; using natural ingredients they help us celebrate the seasons.

SPAGHETTI WITH GRILLED PEPPERS

Serves 4 Freezing recommended for sauce only
Preparation time: 30 minutes + 35 minutes cooking

If you can get it, imported Italian-made pasta is the best kind. The Italians use a hard type of wheat called 'durum' for pasta and all-durum pasta is the only kind that gives a true *al dente* texture. Most pasta in the UK uses a proportion of softer flour but it will work perfectly well in this recipe.

450 g (1 lb) red and/or yellow peppers
5 tablespoons extra virgin olive oil
450 g (1 lb) ripe tomatoes, chopped
2 garlic cloves, chopped finely
2 tablespoons finely chopped fresh parsley
400 g (14 oz) spaghetti
salt and freshly ground black pepper
75 g (2¼ oz) freshly grated Parmesan cheese, to serve

1 Line a baking sheet with foil. Lay the peppers on it in one layer and place under a hot grill. As the skins blacken and blister, turn the peppers over to grill the other sides. Remove from the heat and place in a paper or plastic bag for a few minutes. This helps to steam loose any remaining attached skin. Peel the peppers. In a shallow bowl, pull them open and discard the seeds and stalks. Save the liquid for use in the sauce. Slice the peppers lengthways into thin, narrow strips.

2 Heat 4 tablespoons of the oil in a large heavy skillet. Add the peppers. Season with salt and pepper. Cook over a medium heat for 6–7 minutes, turning the peppers frequently.

3 Slide the peppers into a dish and immediately add the tomatoes to the hot pan with the remaining oil, the garlic and parsley. Season with salt and pepper, stir well and lower the heat slightly. Cook the tomatoes until soft while you bring a large pan of salted water to the boil for the pasta. If the tomatoes begin to dry out add a few tablespoons of the hot pasta-cooking water to them.

4 Add the pasta to the rapidly boiling water. Stir it occasionally. About 5 minutes before the pasta is done, stir the peppers into the tomato sauce with their grilling juices. Stir well and heat through.

5 Drain the pasta when it is still *al dente* (offering a slight resistance to the bite). Add it quickly to the sauce in the skillet. Raise the heat, stir and mix well for 2–3 minutes. Turn into a warmed serving bowl. Serve immediately, passing the cheese separately.

GRATIN OF RED RADICCHIO

Serves 6 as a side dish Freezing not recommended
Preparation time: 40 minutes + 25 minutes baking

In the Veneto region of Italy, around Venice, *radicchio di Treviso* or *Trevisana* is a staple ingredient. There is even a book dedicated to its cookery which features 627 different ways to prepare it! It is important to note this is the long flat-leafed variety, not the more commonly found curly, round red radicchio, which is fine raw but inedibly bitter when cooked. If you can't find the Treviso variety, substitute chicory in this recipe. Serve with grilled or roasted meats, or with a big mixed salad.

800 g (1 lb 12 oz) long red radicchio di Treviso
60 g (2 oz) smoked pancetta, diced finely
1 tablespoon olive oil
700 ml (1¼ pints) milk
a blade of mace
1 bay leaf
7–8 peppercorns
60 g (2 oz) butter
50 g (1¾ oz) plain flour
60 g (2 oz) freshly grated Parmesan cheese
salt and freshly ground black pepper

1 Preheat the oven to Gas Mark 4/180°C/350°F. Bring a large pan of water to the boil for blanching the radicchio. Rinse the radicchio whole. Trim the root section without cutting through the base of the root (or the vegetables will fall apart during cooking). Cut the radicchio into quarters through the root. Blanch in batches, leaving the vegetables in the water for just one minute after the water returns to the boil. Drain upside-down in a colander; when cool, squeeze any excess water out gently. Lightly butter a 28 x 20 cm (11 x 8-inch) oval, or 30 x 21 cm (12 x 8¼-inch) rectangular gratin dish.

2 In a small non-stick frying-pan, heat the pancetta with the oil over a low heat. Cook, stirring frequently, until the fat is rendered and the meat begins to brown. Remove from the heat.

3 Meanwhile, heat the milk with the mace, bay leaf and peppercorns in a small saucepan over a low heat. When it reaches simmering point, remove from the heat.

4 Melt the butter in a medium saucepan. Stir in the flour and cook for 2–3 minutes over a low heat, stirring with a wooden spoon. Pour the hot milk in through a strainer, using a wire whisk to beat the mixture until smooth. Stir constantly until it reaches the boil and bubbles for a couple of minutes. Stir in the pancetta and its fat. Stir in half of the cheese. Taste for seasoning, adding salt and pepper as necessary.

5 Spoon a little of the sauce into the bottom of the gratin dish. Arrange the radicchio over it in one tight layer. Pour on the rest of the béchamel, pushing it down between the radicchio sections. Sprinkle with the remaining cheese, dot with butter and bake for 25 minutes, or until the top is golden and the sauce is bubbling hot.

PESTO LASAGNE WITH BEANS AND POTATOES

Serves 6–8 Freezing recommended
Preparation time: 1 hour + 25 minutes baking

450 g (1 lb) green beans, topped and tailed
450 g (1 lb) potatoes, peeled
400 g (14 oz) fresh egg pasta sheets
85 g (3 oz) Parmesan cheese, freshly grated
8–10 fresh basil leaves
50 g (1¾ oz) pine kernels
butter

FOR THE BÉCHAMEL:

1 litre (1¾ pints) milk
3 blades of mace
2 bay leaves
7 or 8 peppercorns
115 g (4 oz) butter
60 g (2 oz) plain flour
¾ teaspoon salt

FOR THE PESTO:

65 g (2¼ oz) fresh basil leaves
3–4 garlic cloves
50 g (1¾ oz) pine kernels
½ teaspoon salt
5 tablespoons extra virgin olive oil
60 g (2 oz) Parmesan cheese, grated
freshly ground black pepper

1 Blanch the beans in a large pan of boiling water. Lift out with a slotted spoon and refresh under cold water. Set aside. Cook the potatoes until they are barely tender. Cut into 5 mm (¼-inch) slices, when cool.

2 Heat the milk with the mace, bay leaves and peppercorns, in a saucepan set over low heat. When it reaches simmering point, remove from the heat.

3 Melt the butter in a medium-sized saucepan. Add the flour and cook for 2–3 minutes over a low heat, stirring with a wooden spoon. Pour in the hot milk through a strainer, using a wire whisk to beat the mixture until smooth. Add the salt. Stir constantly until the sauce reaches the boil and bubbles for a couple of minutes. Taste for seasoning. Remove from the heat and dot the top with butter, to prevent a skin from forming.

4 If making fresh pesto, combine all the ingredients in the bowl of a food processor or blender and whizz to a paste. Stir the ingredients and push them down the sides of the bowl, to help distribute them evenly.

5 Preheat the oven to Gas Mark 5/190°C/375°F. Butter a large gratin dish or rectangular baking dish (oval 36 x 27 cm/14 x 10½ inches or rectangular 40 x 25 cm/16 x 10 inches). Fit the pasta sheets to the size of the dish, trimming where necessary. Boil them as directed on the package. Spread the pasta out on clean tea-towels.

6 Spoon a little of the béchamel sauce in the bottom of the dish. Cover with a layer of pasta, trimming any edges that come up the sides of the dish. Spoon a little of the pesto over the pasta in a very thin layer. Add about half of the green beans in one even layer. Spoon over some béchamel. Sprinkle with cheese. Add another layer of pasta and a thin layer of pesto. Cover with potato slices in one layer. Spoon over some béchamel. Sprinkle with cheese and half of the pine kernels and a few of the basil leaves, torn into small pieces. Repeat with layers of pasta, beans (or beans and potatoes to

finish them off), pesto, béchamel, cheese. Cover with a final layer of pasta. Dot with more basil pieces. Cover with the remaining béchamel. Sprinkle with the remaining pine kernels and cheese. Dot with butter.

7 Place in the centre of the oven and bake for 25 minutes or until the top is nicely golden and the béchamel is bubbling throughout. Serve directly from the gratin dish.

N O T E : This dish can be prepared the day before.

This beautiful yellow winter-vegetable stew is fragrant with the spices of North Africa. It makes a substantial all-in-one meal and is suitable for dinner parties, as it can be prepared in advance. Cut all the vegetables into good-sized chunks, so they do not break up during cooking. If you like hot condiments, you can also serve the couscous with a fiery harissa sauce, made by diluting a little harissa paste in warm stock and adding a squeeze of lemon and a spoonful of olive oil.

VEGETABLE COUSCOUS WITH PISTACHIO-CORIANDER SAUCE

Serves 8 Freezing not recommended
Preparation time: 40 minutes + 1 hour cooking

40 g (1½ oz) butter

2 tablespoons olive oil

3 onions, cut into eighths through the root

a generous pinch of saffron threads

1 cinnamon stick, broken in two

½ teaspoon ground turmeric

½ teaspoon ground ginger

½ teaspoon ground black pepper

1 small red chilli, chopped, or ¼ teaspoon cayenne pepper

3 tomatoes, peeled and chopped

700 ml (1¼ pints) water, vegetable or chicken stock

1 teaspoon salt

2 tablespoons chopped fresh parsley

2 tablespoons chopped fresh coriander

2 small turnips, cut into eighths

4 parsnips, cut into 4 pieces

3 carrots, cut into 5 or 6 pieces

half a small swede, cut into chunks

2 medium-sized courgettes, cut into 4 or 5 pieces

½ acorn squash, peeled, de-seeded and cut into chunks

*40 g (1½ oz) raisins, soaked for 10 minutes in a little
    hot water*

400 g (14 oz) can of chick-peas, rinsed and drained

FOR THE PISTACHIO-CORIANDER SAUCE:

125 g (4½ oz) unsalted pistachios, shelled

3 tablespoons extra virgin olive oil

1 garlic clove

juice of ½ lemon

4 tablespoons chopped fresh coriander

a small piece of fresh red chilli (optional)

FOR THE COUSCOUS:

500 ml (18 fl oz) water

25 g (1 oz) butter

½ teaspoon salt

500 g (1 lb 2 oz) couscous

1 In a large round casserole, heat the butter with the oil. Stir in the onions and cook over a low heat until they soften, about 7–8 minutes. Add the spices and chilli and mix well. Cook for 1–2 minutes more.

2 Raise the heat to medium and add the chopped tomatoes, water or stock, salt and fresh herbs. Bring to the boil and cook for 5 minutes. Stir in the root vegetables, cover and cook for about 10 minutes.

3 Add the courgettes, squash, raisins and chick-peas. Stir well. Cover and cook for 15 minutes more, or until the vegetables are tender. Taste the sauce for seasoning.

4 Meanwhile, make the sauce. Soak the pistachios in a small bowl of boiling water for about 10 minutes, to soften the dark bitter inner skin. Peel off the skin and place the nuts in the bowl of a food processor or blender with the remaining sauce ingredients. Process as you would a pesto. Turn into a small bowl, cover and chill until required.

5 Just before serving, prepare the couscous. Heat the water with 200 ml (7 fl oz) of cooking juices from the vegetables. When it boils, pour it into a large warmed bowl. Add the butter and salt, and stir in the couscous. Cover the bowl and allow to stand for about 7–8 minutes. Use a fork to fluff the couscous grains before serving. Serve, passing the sauce separately.

AUBERGINE CAPONATA

Serves 4 Freezing not recommended
Preparation and cooking time: 10 minutes + 1 hour draining + 50 minutes

Originally an elaborate Spanish dish containing shellfish as well as vegetables, the modern version of this sweet and sour Sicilian favourite features aubergines, almonds and celery.

750 g (1 lb 10 oz) firm, shiny aubergines
40 g (1½ oz) sultanas
2 tablespoons extra virgin olive oil
1 onion, sliced finely
225 g (8 oz) plum tomatoes, peeled, de-seeded and
*   chopped finely*
2 tablespoons capers, rinsed
4–5 tender, central stalks of celery, sliced into 2 cm
*   (¾-inch) pieces*
75 g (2¾ oz) green or Riviera olives, stoned
½ teaspoon ground black pepper
¼ teaspoon ground cinnamon
oil for deep-frying
2 tablespoons sugar
125 ml (4 fl oz) white wine vinegar
10 blanched almonds, split
3 tablespoons chopped fresh basil
salt

1 Scrub the aubergines and cut them into 2 cm (¾-inch) cubes. Sprinkle with salt and place in a colander set on a draining board. Leave to drain for an hour. Soak the sultanas in a small bowl of warm water. Leave to plump for about 30 minutes before draining.

2 Heat the oil in a medium casserole or sauté pan. Stir in the onion and cook until soft and golden, 10–12 minutes. Stir in the tomatoes and cook over a medium heat for 3–4 minutes. Add the capers, celery, olives and spices. Cook for a further 10–12 minutes.

3 Meanwhile, rinse the salted aubergine pieces quickly in cold water. Pat them dry, using paper towels. Heat the frying oil to 185°C/360°F or until a cube of day-old bread browns in 30 seconds. Deep-fry the aubergine cubes, in batches, until golden. Drain on paper towels.

4 Add the aubergines to the sauce with the sugar, vinegar and almonds. Simmer until the vinegar evaporates and the sauce reduces slightly. Remove from the heat and stir in the basil. Season to taste. Serve the caponata at room temperature or chilled, as an *antipasto* or side dish.

MEDITERRANEAN CHICK-PEA STEW

Serves 5 as a side dish Freezing recommended
Preparation and cooking time: 45 minutes

Canned chick-peas are nutritious staples for the store cupboard. This recipe dresses them with a spicy sauce. They are good with roast meats, on pasta or rice, or as one of a group of vegetable dishes. Omit the pancetta for a vegetarian version.

2 red or yellow peppers
100 g (3½ oz) smoked pancetta or bacon, diced
1 tablespoon extra virgin olive oil
2 garlic cloves
2 x 400 g (14 oz) cans of chick-peas, rinsed and
  drained
FOR THE SAUCE:
2 tablespoons extra virgin olive oil
1 medium onion, chopped finely
400 g (14 oz) can of peeled plum tomatoes plus their
  juices
¼ teaspoon or more hot pepper sauce (optional)
a few fresh basil leaves
salt and freshly ground black pepper

1 Preheat the grill to hot and grill the peppers, turning from time to time, until the skin is black and blistered all over. Leave to cool in a plastic bag, which will make them easier to peel. Remove the skins and discard the seeds.

2 Place the pancetta in a small, heavy frying-pan with the oil and garlic, and cook over a low heat until the meat renders its fat and begins to turn light brown. Discard the garlic. Remove the pan from the heat and set aside.

3 Meanwhile, make the sauce. Heat the oil in a saucepan or casserole. Add the onion and cook over a medium to low heat until it softens, about 10 minutes. Add the tomatoes and their juice. Raise the heat slightly and cook for 5 minutes. Season with salt and pepper.

4 Using a food processor or hand-held blender, whizz the sauce, adding the peeled peppers, pepper sauce and basil leaves. Purée until smooth.

5 Combine the sauce, the chick-peas and the pancetta with its oil in a medium-sized heavy saucepan. Heat slowly, stirring often, until the mixture comes back to the boil and the chick-peas are heated through. Taste and adjust the seasoning before serving.

NOTE: You can substitute bottled or canned pimientos, as long as they have not been preserved in vinegar.

COURGETTE BAKE WITH RICE AND MARJORAM

Serves 6 Freezing not recommended
Preparation time: 45 minutes + 25 minutes baking

1 kg (2 lb 4 oz) courgettes
125 g (4½ oz) long-grain rice
about 400 ml (14 fl oz) milk
3 tablespoons extra virgin olive oil
1 onion, chopped finely
3 garlic cloves, chopped finely
2 tablespoons plain flour
60 g (2 oz) Parmesan cheese, grated
¼ teaspoon grated nutmeg or mace
1 tablespoon or more chopped fresh marjoram or basil
2 tablespoons dried white breadcrumbs
25 g (1 oz) butter
salt and freshly ground black pepper

1 Using the coarse setting on a grater or food processor, grate the courgettes into a large bowl. Sprinkle with salt and leave for 5 minutes.

2 Cook the rice in a pan of boiling water for 5 minutes. Drain and set aside. Butter a gratin dish (the oval 32 x 23 cm/12½ x 9 inches size works perfectly).

3 Take a large handful of the grated courgettes and, holding it over another bowl, squeeze it firmly between both hands until the juice runs out. Put the squeezed courgettes into a third bowl and continue until all the courgettes have been squeezed. Pour the green liquid into a measuring jug and add milk to bring the volume up to 625 ml (just over 1 pint). Pour into a small pan and bring to a simmer.

4 Preheat the oven to Gas Mark 7/220°C/425°F. In a large skillet, heat the oil. Add the onion and cook over a medium heat until it is soft and golden, about 10 minutes. Stir in the garlic and cook for a minute more. Add the squeezed courgettes and cook, stirring, for 6–7 minutes.

5 Stir the flour into the vegetables. Pour in the hot milk mixture and bring to the simmering point, stirring to blend the flour and liquids together. Remove from the heat and add the cooked rice and the cheese. Season with nutmeg or mace and black pepper. Taste for saltiness. Stir in the fresh herbs. (Taste a leaf of the marjoram: if it is very highly perfumed, 1 tablespoon may suffice. If it is milder, or if you are using basil, add more.)

6 Turn the mixture into the prepared gratin dish. Sprinkle with the breadcrumbs and dot the top with butter. Bake in the hot oven for about 25 minutes or until the top is golden.

THE LAND

The land is always bounteous. Around the
Mediterranean it provides sweet-scented pastures for
sheep and goats to graze in; their aromatic cheeses –
pecorino, ricotta, chèvre – are fragrant from its wild
herbs. The woods and hills harbour game and fowl
whose meat is enriched by the sweet fruits that grow
wild: green and black figs and all kinds of wild berries.

SLICED CHICKEN BREASTS WITH OLIVE-PASTE SAUCE

Serves 2–3 Freezing not recommended
Preparation time: 10 minutes + 15 minutes cooking

This is a quick way to jazz up a chicken breast; it makes an easy supper dish. Use as good a commercial olive paste as you can find: some of the poorer quality pastes also contain anchovy and taste quite bitter.

2 boneless, skinless chicken breasts
25 g (1 oz) butter
2 tablespoons olive oil
FOR THE SAUCE:
200 ml (7 fl oz) chicken stock
3 tablespoons black olive paste
2 tablespoons crème fraîche
salt and freshly ground black pepper

1 Lay the chicken breasts on a cutting board. Place your hand on top of one and, using your hand as a guide, slice the breast horizontally into three or four flat slices. Repeat with the other breast.

2 In a large skillet or sauté pan, heat the butter with the oil. When the butter is foaming, add as many slices of chicken as will fit in one layer. Cook over a medium heat until the chicken is just golden, about 2–3 minutes per side. Remove to a heated plate. Cook the remaining chicken slices, transferring them to the hot plate when done. Season with a little salt and pepper.

3 Pour the stock into the hot pan, scraping up the cooking juices and particles. Cook for a few minutes, until it has been reduced by about one-third. Stir in the olive paste, blending it well with the stock. Cook for 2 minutes more. Add the crème fraîche and heat to simmering point. Serve the chicken immediately, with a little sauce spooned on to each plate.

CHICKEN SAUTÉ WITH FENNEL AND SHALLOTS

Serves 4 Freezing recommended
Preparation and cooking time: 1¼ hours

Unlike a stew, a sauté uses very little liquid. The natural flavour of the bird is enhanced by the cooking method, so be sure to use very fresh (preferably free-range) chicken, which will have lots of flavour. Serve with rice or noodles.

3 fennel bulbs
5 tablespoons extra virgin olive oil
300 g (10½ oz) shallots, skinned, roots trimmed but not cut off
8 or 9 chicken pieces, thighs and/or drumsticks
2 garlic cloves, chopped
150 ml (¼ pint) dry white wine
2 tablespoons fresh lemon juice
salt and freshly ground black pepper

1 Bring a large saucepan of water to the boil. Trim the feathery fronds from the top of the fennel and reserve. Remove any very tough, stringy outer leaves (use them later in a soup). Quarter the bulbs through the base, retaining enough of the root section to hold the layers together. When the water is boiling, blanch the fennel for 4 minutes after the water comes back to the boil. Lift out of the water using a slotted spoon (the cooking water is good for soup, too).

2 Heat 3 tablespoons of the oil in a sauté pan or buffet casserole. Add the fennel and shallots and cook gently until just golden on all sides, about 20 minutes, turning frequently. Lift the vegetables out of the pan and transfer to a bowl.

3 Trim any excess fat from the chicken pieces. Season with salt and pepper. Add 2 more tablespoons of the oil to the pan. Arrange the chicken in one layer and brown on all sides. This will take about 6–7 minutes per side.

4 Return the vegetables to the pan, tucking them in under the chicken in an even layer. Sprinkle with the garlic. Cover the pan (the lid of the 30 cm/12-inch buffet casserole fits the sauté pan perfectly; or you can use foil). Cook over a low heat for about 30 minutes, or until the drumstick juices run clear when pricked with a fork. Shake the pan frequently as you cook, turning the vegetables occasionally.

5 When the chicken is done, arrange it on a heated platter with the vegetables. Pour the wine and lemon juice into the pan to deglaze it. Spoon the sauce over the chicken. Sprinkle with some of the reserved fennel fronds.

RED PEPPER SOUFFLÉ

Serves 4 Freezing not recommended
Preparation time: 1 hour + 25 minutes baking

These days, with egg beaters in every home, making a soufflé is a lot less tricky than it used to be. In fact, it's hard for them to go wrong – even if they don't rise much, the taste will be great and few other recipes can compare for sheer spectacle. However, avoid trying soufflés in ovens with top-heat sources only; for the mixture to rise, it needs steady heat from the sides and/or from below. Have the eggs at room temperature and measure your ingredients carefully. That's all there is to it!

2 red peppers
about 250 ml (9 fl oz) milk
75 g (2¾ oz) grated Parmesan or Swiss cheese
2 shallots, chopped finely
1 tablespoon olive oil or 15 g (½ oz) butter
½ teaspoon dried herbs, e.g. oregano, thyme or herbes
  de Provence
1 blade of mace
1 bay leaf
a few peppercorns
25 g (1 oz) butter
40 g (1½ oz) plain flour
5 eggs
salt and freshly ground black pepper

1 Preheat the grill to hot. Cook the peppers under the grill, turning them occasionally, until black and blistered on all sides. Transfer them to a plastic or paper bag for 5 minutes before peeling. Discard the stems and seeds. Pour any cooking juices into a measuring jug, adding enough milk to make 250 ml (9 fl oz). Weigh the peppers. You will need 200 g (7 oz). (Save any extra for use in salads or sandwiches.) Dice the peppers.

2 Set the oven temperature at Gas Mark 5/190°C/375°F. Generously butter a 20 x 10 cm (8 x 4-inch) soufflé dish. Sprinkle in about a tablespoon of the grated cheese, rolling the dish around in your hands until all the cheese has stuck to the butter. Shake out any excess cheese.

3 In a small saucepan, cook the shallots gently with the oil or butter until they soften, 4–5 minutes. Stir in the peppers, add the dried herbs, season with salt and pepper and cook for about 5 minutes. Stir often or the peppers will stick. Remove from the heat and set aside.

4 In another small saucepan, bring the milk and pepper juices gently to simmering point with the mace, bay leaf and peppercorns. Remove from the heat and allow to infuse until needed.

5 In a medium-sized saucepan or casserole, heat the butter. When it has melted, stir in the flour with a wooden spoon. Cook for 1–2 minutes, stirring. Pour the hot milk mixture in through a strainer. Stir vigorously with a small whisk until the sauce is thick, smooth and bubbling. This won't take long. Remove from the heat and immediately separate the first egg, dropping the white into a large clean mixing bowl and the yolk into the hot sauce. Stir well. Repeat with 3 more eggs. Stir the pepper mixture and all but 2 tablespoons of the cheese into the sauce. Season with salt and pepper to taste. Set aside.

6 Add one more egg white to the others in the bowl (discard the fifth egg yolk). Add a pinch of salt. Using an electric or hand whisk, beat them until they form very stiff peaks.

7 Stir about one-quarter of the egg whites into the béchamel mixture. This will lighten its consistency. Slide the remaining egg whites into the mixture and, using a rubber spatula or large metal spoon, carefully fold the egg whites in. With each stroke, cut down to the bottom of the pan to bring up the sauce at the bottom without deflating the beaten egg whites. When the two are fairly well amalgamated (do not over-fold) turn the mixture into the prepared soufflé dish. Sprinkle with the remaining cheese and immediately place in the centre of the hot oven. Quickly close the door and do not re-open again until the soufflé is done, 25–30 minutes. You will know when it is done because it will have browned on top and risen. Serve immediately, directly from the soufflé dish.

HERB-MARINATED GRILLED LAMB STEAKS

Serves 4 Freezing not recommended
Preparation time: 5 minutes + marinating + grilling

If you have only 5 minutes to spare, a few hours before mealtime, this marinade can make the difference between a plain dinner and a deliciously aromatic one. It works equally well with lamb or pork chops. You should marinate the meat for 3 hours or longer – it will only improve the flavour. Use a Le Creuset Grillit pan, kitchen grill or barbecue.

4 lamb steaks, trimmed of excess fat
FOR THE MARINADE:
juice of 1 lemon
1 tablespoon balsamic vinegar
4 tablespoons extra virgin olive oil
2 garlic cloves, chopped
1 teaspoon juniper berries, crushed lightly
½ teaspoon coarsely crushed black peppercorns
a handful of mixed fresh garden herbs, e.g. parsley, sage, rosemary and thyme, or any others you prefer, chopped

1 In a shallow non-metallic bowl or gratin dish, combine all the marinade ingredients, including the herbs. Pat the steaks dry before putting them into the marinade. Turn them all around until some of the dressing is on each side of the meat and the aromatic ingredients are well distributed. Cover the dish and refrigerate. If possible, turn the meat after about 2 hours.

2 Preheat the Grillit, grill or barbecue. Grill the steaks until golden on one side. Turn, spoon on any remaining marinade and continue cooking until the meat is cooked the way you like it. Serve at once.

SPICED MEATBALLS WITH PEAS

Serves 4 as a main course Freezing recommended
Preparation time: 35 minutes + 30 minutes cooking

These meatballs can be served with their sauce over rice as a main course, by themselves as party appetisers, or as part of a selection of tapas dishes.

FOR THE MEATBALLS:
1 medium onion, grated
250 g (9 oz) minced pork or lamb
450 g (1 lb) minced beef
1½ teaspoons salt
¼ teaspoon ground cumin
¼ teaspoon ground coriander
a pinch of grated nutmeg
¼ teaspoon ground black peppercorns
2 tablespoons finely chopped fresh parsley
5 tablespoons dried white breadcrumbs
1 tablespoon fresh lemon juice
1 egg, beaten
plain flour, for rolling
3 tablespoons extra virgin olive oil
FOR THE SAUCE:
1 tablespoon extra virgin olive oil
1 small onion, chopped finely
125 ml (4 fl oz) white wine
2 garlic cloves, chopped
250 g (9 oz) tomatoes, chopped
250 ml (9 fl oz) water
225 g (8 oz) fresh or frozen peas
salt and freshly ground black pepper

1 In a large mixing bowl, combine all the meatball ingredients, up to and including the egg. Mix well. Using your fingers, form little meatballs about 4 cm (1½ inches) across. Roll them in flour, dusting off the excess.

2 In a large skillet, sauté pan or buffet casserole, heat the olive oil. Add the meatballs in one layer and brown them on all sides over a medium heat, turning them frequently. As they brown, remove the meatballs to a side plate using a slotted spoon.

3 To make the sauce, add the olive oil to the same pan with the onion. Lower the heat and cook, stirring constantly, until it softens. Pour in the wine and cook until it reduces by about half. Add the garlic, tomatoes and water and cook for 7–8 minutes.

4 If you like your sauce chunky, add the peas and meat-balls now. If you prefer a smoother sauce, pour it into a blender or food processor, purée, and return it to the pan. Then add the peas and meatballs. Taste for and adjust the seasoning. Cook for 15 minutes, turning the meatballs occasionally. Serve hot.

This is a classic combination, flavoured here with Provençal herbs. The lamb is cooked in a rich gravy, which is spooned over the beans. Serve with crusty bread to mop up the juices, and a tossed green salad.

LAMB STEW WITH WHITE BEANS

Serves 6—8 Freezing recommended. Preparation time, beans: overnight soaking + 2 hours preparation and cooking; lamb: 35 minutes preparation + 1½–2 hours cooking

3-4 tablespoons extra virgin olive oil

1 kg (2 lb 4 oz) lean shoulder of lamb, boned and cubed, bones chopped into 3 or 4 pieces and reserved, or stewing lamb, cubed

75 g (2¾ oz) plain flour

500 ml (18 fl oz) dry white wine

400 g (14 oz) can of peeled plum tomatoes, chopped, plus their juice, or unseasoned, canned chopped tomatoes

875 ml (1 pint 11 fl oz) water

600 g (1 lb 5 oz) red onions, chopped finely

1 small celery stick, sliced finely

2 carrots, sliced finely

1 garlic clove, chopped

2 tablespoons chopped fresh parsley

a few sprigs of fresh thyme or ½ teaspoon dried thyme

½ teaspoon dried oregano

1 bay leaf

salt and freshly ground black pepper

2–3 tablespoons finely chopped fresh parsley, to serve

FOR THE BEANS:

600 g (1 lb 5 oz) cannellini or haricot beans, soaked in cold water for 8 hours or overnight

2 tablespoons extra virgin olive oil

75 g (2¾ oz) smoked bacon or pancetta, diced

3 carrots, sliced finely

2 medium onions, chopped finely

2 bay leaves

3 tablespoons chopped fresh parsley

a few sprigs of fresh thyme or ½ teaspoon dried

2 teaspoons salt

1 Drain and rinse the beans. Place in a large saucepan or casserole and cover with water. Bring to the boil and cook for 10 minutes. Drain.

2 In a large, heavy casserole (about 22 cm/8½ inches in diameter), heat the oil with the bacon or pancetta. Cook for 5–6 minutes or until just golden. Add the vegetables and cover the pan. Cook for 7–8 minutes more. Add the beans and enough water just to cover them. Stir in the herbs and cook, partly covered for 1½–2 hours, or until the beans are tender. Cooking times vary greatly, depending on the freshness and type of the beans. Add the salt and reserve the beans until needed.

3 In another large casserole, heat 3 tablespoons of the oil. Stir in enough lamb pieces and bones to make one layer. Brown over a medium heat, turning the meat to brown it evenly on all sides. Remove to a side dish, using a slotted spoon. Add another batch of lamb, plus a bit more oil, if necessary. Repeat until all the lamb has been browned. Return all the meat to the pan, lower the heat slightly and add the flour, stirring it all around.

4 Pour in the wine. Bring to the boil, stirring well to amalgamate it with the flour. Add the tomatoes and their juices and the water. Bring to the boil. Stir in the vegetables and herbs. Cover the pan and leave to simmer.

5 After about 30 minutes, taste the sauce, adding salt and pepper as necessary. Then cook for another hour or so until the lamb is tender, stirring occasionally. Serve accompanied by the beans, which should be warmed before serving, and spoon some of the lamb gravy over them. Sprinkle each plate lightly with parsley.

After a meal of bright colours and flavours, the most refreshing, simplest solution is to place a painterly bowl of fresh fruit in the centre of the table and let everybody help themselves. Select healthy ripe fruits with fine colours and arrange them in a pretty dish over a few leaves (fig, fern or wisteria work well) clipped from the garden. Pass a bowl of cool water to rinse the fruit in. Nothing else recalls the experience of ending a meal in the Mediterranean quite as vividly.

If whole fruit seems too mundane a dessert, there are lots of easy ways to dress it up by adding one or two simple ingredients. A list of ideas of how to do this can be found opposite. I have also included two recipes for what I like to think of as 'building blocks': a plain lemon-scented cake, and a basic sorbet. They go very well with fruit in any of its guises and are good alone, too.

TO FINISH

SOME DELICIOUS WAYS TO FINISH A MEDITERRANEAN MEAL

FIGS are one of the greatest fruits, if you are lucky enough to find them fresh and ripe. If eating them raw isn't fancy enough, they can be quartered, topped with a little honey and whipped cream and grilled until golden. Or try eating them plain with some crunchy French bread for breakfast.

WINE plays an important role in Mediterranean fruit desserts. Poaching pears in red wine is a classic, but other combinations work well too: prunes take on a new dimension when stewed in red wine, as do apples. Peaches are delicious peeled, stoned and sliced into glasses of wine, as are strawberries (though these are perhaps better with just a squeeze of lemon and a sprinkling of sugar on them).

HONEY is a key Mediterranean ingredient. The lavender fields of Provence are legendary, as is their honey, but be on the lookout for chestnut honey also. It has a more pronounced taste and an amber transparency that is well suited to cooking. Stir it into cream, soft cheeses or yogurt. Eat it with cheese or use it to flavour vanilla ice cream.

RICOTTA CHEESE can be sweetened by beating a little sugar or honey into it. Make it even more exotic by adding a few drops of rose- or orange-flower water, or a few tablespoons of chopped, candied fruits. Serve with stewed winter fruit or fresh berries. In Italy or Spain the most exquisite ricotta cheese is made from sheep's milk – its distinctive fragrance comes from the aromatic herb pastures used for grazing.

PECORINO is a sheep's milk cheese. In Tuscany it is classically served with pears, but is also good with a few walnuts and a little well-flavoured honey drizzled over it. Pecorino varies from creamy and mild to hard and tangy – choose the one you like best. To serve pecorino for a dinner party, fan peeled slices of perfectly ripe pears on plates and arrange thin slices of pecorino on top. If you drizzle on a few drops of extra virgin olive oil, you could serve this as a starter.

MASCARPONE is a very rich cream cheese. Its most famous role is in tiramisù, but it can be good sweetened with caster sugar or honey and a little rum or marsala. Serve with a hot compote of fruit or with fine biscuits.

QUINCE CHEESE isn't a cheese at all, but a rich sticky paste of the fruit much favoured in Spain. It is great cut into little cubes and served with fromage frais.

AMARETTI biscuits are, along with cantucci (the almond biscotti dipped into Vin Santo) Italy's most popular after-dinner biscuits. The Saronno type come in very fine paper wrappings that make a spectacular end to a dinner party: after eating the amaretti, roll the paper into a tube shape. Stand on a plate and light the top end with a match. Then turn off the lights.

PEACHES are transformed by cooking. For 4 people soak 60 g (2 oz) crushed amaretti biscuits in 2 tablespoons of marsala wine or sweet sherry. Stir in 1 egg yolk and 1 tablespoon of sugar and a few drops of vanilla extract. Use to fill the hollows of 4 halved peaches. Dot with butter and arrange in a gratin dish in one layer. Bake for about 30 minutes at Gas Mark 5/190°C/375°F and serve hot or cold with some sweetened mascarpone.

MACEDONIA is Italian for fruit salad. Use any fresh fruit; cut it into bite-sized pieces and put it with its juice in a serving bowl. Pour over the juice of one or two oranges. Adjust the sweetness and sharpness to your taste with sugar and lemon juice. Mix well, cover and allow to stand in a cool place for at least 30 minutes before serving.

LEMON-SCENTED CAKE

Serves 8 Freezing recommended

Preparation time: 40 minutes + 30 minutes baking

This compact, fragrant cake is quick to make and goes well with fresh fruit or fruit salad. Its lemony sharpness offers a nice way to end a meal of decisive Mediterranean flavours.

140 g (5 oz) butter

140 g (5 oz) sugar

2 eggs

125 g (4½ oz) plain flour

1 teaspoon baking powder

juice and finely grated rind of 1 lemon, scrubbed before grating

1 teaspoon vanilla extract

salt

FOR THE ICING:

15 g (½ oz) unsalted butter

3 tablespoons freshly squeezed lemon juice

140 g (5 oz) icing sugar, sifted

1 Have all the cake ingredients at room temperature before you begin. Preheat the oven to Gas Mark 4/180°C/350°F. Butter a 20 cm (8-inch) round or small rectangular loaf tin, and line the bottom with buttered greaseproof paper.

2 In a mixing bowl, cream the butter with the sugar until pale yellow. Separate the eggs, dropping the whites into another bowl and beating the yolks into the butter mixture, one at a time. Stir in a couple of tablespoons of flour, the lemon juice and rind and the vanilla extract.

3 Sift the remaining flour with the baking powder. Beat the egg whites with a pinch of salt until they form stiff peaks. Fold the egg whites into the butter mixture alternately with the flour. Turn into the prepared tin, spreading the mixture evenly with a spatula. Bake in the centre of the oven for about 30 minutes, or until a fine skewer inserted into the middle of the cake comes out clean. Allow the cake to cool for 5 minutes before turning it on to a wire rack.

4 When the cake is almost cool, make the icing. Place the butter and lemon juice in a small saucepan over a low heat. When the butter has melted, stir in the icing sugar, a little at a time, beating well with a small whisk. Stir for a couple of minutes before removing from the heat. This helps to eliminate the raw flavour that icing sugar often has.

5 Place the cake on a serving plate. Spread or pour the icing over the top. (If it is too thick, add a little more juice; if it is too thin, add a little more sugar.) Allow to cool before serving.

FRUIT SORBET

Serves 6–8 Freezing recommended
Preparation time: 30 minutes + freezing

Nothing is as refreshing or as intensely flavoured as a sorbet. In Sicily, they even make a scented ice from jasmine blossoms. Use sorbets to end your meals or as taste 'punctuation' between courses.

Fresh fruit sorbets are very easy to make, especially if you have an ice-cream machine. If you don't have one, a food processor or powerful blender will still enable you to produce them quite easily. Check the capacity of your ice-cream machine. You may have to halve this recipe.

This is a 'master' recipe that can be adapted to almost any fruit. Use crushed and strained soft fruit (berries, passion-fruit, mango, peach), lightly stewed and strained harder fruit (apple, pear, apricot), or strained juice (lemon, blood orange, pink grapefruit, lime). Combine with the sugar syrup. Adjust the taste with lemon juice or icing sugar. Freeze. The basic rule is: if it tastes good at room temperature, it will taste good frozen!

175 g (6 oz) sugar
125 ml (4 fl oz) water
250 ml (9 fl oz) strained fruit
juice of 1 or 2 lemons
about 375 ml (12½ fl oz) water
    or juice, as needed
sifted icing sugar, as needed

1 Dissolve the sugar in the smaller quantity of water in a small heavy saucepan over a medium heat. Do not stir. Boil for about 2 minutes. Allow to cool.
2 Combine the strained fruit with the sugar syrup. Add the juice of one lemon and about 250 ml (9 fl oz) of water or fruit juice. Taste carefully. Adjust the flavour by adding more lemon juice (which will sharpen it), icing sugar (which will sweeten it), or water (which will dilute it). When you have reached a good balance of sharpness and sweetness, pour into the ice-cream maker and freeze, following the manufacturer's instructions. Or pour into a freezerproof container and freeze; in this case when the sorbet is half frozen, whizz it in a food processor or blender; then return it to the freezer container until set.

INDEX